Keep the Light Burning

Story by Melaina Faranda

Illustrations by Chiara Fedele

Contents

Author's Note

This story is set on Tasman Island, an isolated island off the south-eastern coast of Tasmania, Australia. The events take place in the 1930s, during the Great Depression. This was a time when banks around the world failed, many people became unemployed and many farmers were at risk of losing their farms.

Chapter 1

What's Around the Corner?

"For goodness' sake, children, sit still!" Mother hissed as she cradled the baby who, after hours of grizzling, had finally fallen asleep. She glanced to where Father brooded against the boat rail. "Robert?"

Father reluctantly unstuck his gaze from the ocean and frowned at Henry and Annabelle, who were darting about between teetering piles of boxes, crates, caged chickens, and two confused-looking milking goats. But the children could tell that Father didn't have the heart to scold them.

For all their lives they had only known flat, endless fields, crumbled to dirt by a punishing sun. Even though Henry was eleven and Annabelle twelve, the biggest body of water they had ever seen was their farm's own muddy dam, ringed by parched sheep. Being on a boat, surrounded by the shifting blues and greens of the sea, was thrilling.

They had learnt about the ocean through books, of course, as well as Father's stories about serving in the navy during the Great War, from 1914 to 1918.

The reality of the sea was different from any story, though.

The sea was even more incredible than the first fat drops of rain that had greeted them on the other side of the long train journey from the farm. Rain that had turned into hissing, spitting needles that left both of the children gaping at the sky, too amazed to take cover.

For Henry and Annabelle, rain seemed like showers of precious coins being tossed away. On the farm, they had measured out water drop by drop. Water that had been pumped up from underground and had trickled thin and brown even before each member of the family had taken their turn with a sponge at the wash basin.

Yet Father still hadn't wanted to leave the farm. It was Mother who had warned that if they were not careful, their debt would grow even worse and the bank would take the farm from them. Then Father would have to join the long lines of wandering men with bulky sacks swung over their shoulders, looking for work.

Henry had once been given a sharp scolding for calling these men "hoboes". Their numbers had grown ever since the Great Depression started in 1929. The men's strange bulky shapes, laden down with the sacks they carried, would occasionally appear against the shimmering heat haze of the horizon back at the farm.

Mother had always treated these travellers kindly at the farm gate, inviting them in for tea and quietly explaining to the children that these men had lost everything – their jobs, homes and even their families. She always finished with, "You never know what might come around the corner."

As it turned out, good things could come around the corner, too. Only three weeks ago, Mother had triumphantly waved a letter that said Father's application had been successful. He was to be a lighthouse keeper on a distant island!

"What have you done?" Father had demanded, shaking his head at Mother's story of having seen the advertisement in the newspaper and applying on his behalf. She had calmly explained that the position was for three years and there was no knowing how long the drought would last. This way, they could pay off the bank and save the farm. In a time when so many were suffering, he was fortunate to have been given the job.

It was Mother who had overseen the sale of the last of their dwindling flock of sheep, and the packing of anything and everything that could be useful on an island. Father would be able to teach the children how to swim and fish, and they would all have amazing adventures in a place where they would never run short of water!

Chapter 2

Welcome to Paradise

The ship's horn blared, causing a flock of gulls to rise and shriek irritably as the boat chugged out from the fishing port, across open sea to the lighthouse island.

For Annabelle and Henry, the grand adventure of days on a train, then helping to load the boat, was replaced by the green-faced awfulness of trying not to lose their morning's porridge to the heaving sea.

A crew mate staggered over and offered Father a thin coil of rope. "It's best you tie the children to the boat, so they don't get washed overboard. Skipper says the swell's only going to get worse."

It was rough sailing, and the children clung to their mother as the boat pitched and lurched in the angry grey ocean, until finally a dim mass began to take shape in the distance.

As they drew closer, the island loomed above them through rearing waves and seething white froth. Gulls soared overhead, piercing the sea's booming with their melancholy cries. There were no coves or beaches or trees on the island. There was a jagged platform of rock, strewn with seals, and dark sheer cliffs rising into white cloud so thick that it was impossible to see the lighthouse.

Part-way up the cliff, on a narrow wedge of bright emerald grass, a man in an oilskin coat operated a winch for a flying fox: a big basket hanging from a long cable. Already, two of the men from the boat had taken a smaller dinghy over to retrieve the line.

The boat bobbed close to the treacherous rocks as the enormous square basket was winched down.

"Women and children first," one of the crew barked over the wind, motioning to the basket. He gave the children a wink as Mother's face turned white.

"I'll go," Annabelle bravely volunteered.

Father smiled grimly. "We'll all go together. And the goats."

They clambered into the basket along with two unhappy goats, despite the very real threat of a wave rearing up to slap them all sideways and tip them into the freezing sea.

Annabelle slipped her hand around Henry's trembling fingers. "Remember," she said, "it's an adventure."

Within moments, her smile vanished as the basket swung above the sea – rising higher and higher on the cable and swinging violently in the wind.

When they reached the patch of grass on the cliff, the man operating the cable greeted the family with a wild grin. The children saw that there was something that glittered too brightly in his eyes.

"Welcome to paradise! I'm the outgoing lighthouse keeper. I will be handing over and showing you your duties over the next few days."

He pointed to another basket and then straight up to the swirling blanket of mist. "You're almost there."

There was still another flying fox to the top.

Chapter 3

Some Getting Used To

By the time they reached the top of the island, everyone was thoroughly soaked from sea spray and squalls of rain.

Father and the lighthouse keeper went straight to the tall, white lighthouse, for the man was eager to show Father all that he knew. Henry and Annabelle also longed to climb the tower and peer out through its immense glass lantern room. Instead, they were directed to accompany Mother to a whitewashed stone cottage squatting a short distance from the lighthouse.

At the cottage, they were greeted by the lighthouse keeper's wife and a gaggle of children with pink-rimmed eyes and running noses. The pale, worn-looking woman waggled floury fingers and clucked admiringly over the baby.

Henry and Annabelle saw how their mother's sharp gaze passed over the mouldy window ledges and the mud-scuffed timber floors. There was an unpleasant odour of fried fat and wet wool.

"This will be your cottage," the woman explained, wiping her hands on her apron. "The children and I have made scones for you. I'm sorry that we have no cream to go with them, but recently our cow –"

She was interrupted by an unhappy gasp from one of the children.

"Well," the woman continued, looking squarely at Mother, "the wind can blow so fierce here that let's just say it has sometimes been necessary for me to tie all the children together with a rope, lest they be blown over the cliff's edge."

Mother gave a quiet laugh, then stopped as she saw the woman had spoken with complete seriousness.

"The other thing you'll find," the woman continued, passing around mugs of tea without milk, "is that no matter how well you keep the fire burning, the cottage will always be damp."

Henry bit into a scone and gagged. There was something oily and fishy tasting about it.

The lighthouse keeper's wife smiled. "It can take some getting used to mutton bird eggs."

Secretly spitting the mouthful of scone into his hand, Henry hoped the ginger cat stalking below the table would relieve him of it.

The woman turned back to Mother. “It is good that you will be here with your husband and busy with your baby and children,” she said. “The owner of the lighthouse won’t employ single men as lighthouse keepers. It’s thought that the loneliness can do strange things to their heads.”

She glanced worriedly through the mist-beaded window towards the lighthouse and added quietly, “But even a man with a wife and children can suffer.”

The family slept that night on thin mattresses in the parlour, listening to the outgoing lighthouse keeper's children coughing throughout the night, as the wind howled against the cottage walls, rattling the glass panes and peeling at the corners of the iron roof.

So, although the hour was late and the oil lamp was turned low, Annabelle and Henry both heard Mother whisper to Father, "What have I done?"

Chapter 4

Mutton Bird Eggs for Breakfast

Back on the farm, Father had risen with the first birdsong, and frequently did not return to the house before dark. There had always been something to tend to – fencing to be mended, animals to be fed and cared for, equipment to be fixed.

Now, despite being on an island, and in the most opposite place imaginable to the farm, living creatures – this time, humans – continued to rely on Father.

Mother had impressed upon the children that being a lighthouse keeper was a very important job. Lighthouses were necessary to save boats and ships from wrecking themselves against the rocks. The slow-turning beam swept through mist and fog, skimming the sea to ensure the safety of hundreds – even thousands – of souls, as they glided by unharmed in their ships.

Father's most important duty was to tend to the lighthouse lantern at night, to ensure that the light shone strong and clear.

During the day, Father's duties included cleaning and polishing the lens, along with the great windows of the circular lantern room at the very top of the tower. He took daily weather readings and recorded all the lighthouse activities.

Each morning, Father allowed Henry and Annabelle into the lighthouse with him to help sweep the floors and stairs of dust. He was forever painting or oiling, and it seemed that no sooner had a section of paint been dried by the wind, than it peeled in the salt spray and he had to start it again.

Mother insisted that the goats be firmly tethered to stakes pounded into the ground. She would not let them wander over the island in case they met the same fate as the previous family's cow.

The chickens were another matter, however. Although their feathers had been clipped, Annabelle called to Henry one day as the wind snatched up a chicken and sent it sailing across the width of the island. They found it much later, dazed and hunkered beneath a spindly bush. Henry tucked the chicken under his arm, from where it issued the occasional confused and mournful cluck. Soon after this, the chickens stopped laying and there were no more eggs.

"What about the mutton bird eggs?" Annabelle asked.

It was a bad day when Mother finally brought herself to crack two mutton bird eggs into the pan.

Living on the island had been fine at the start, when the supply boat had come more regularly. Along with fuel for the lighthouse, the boat brought vegetables and fruits, including potatoes, pumpkins, carrots and apples. But when the weather was bad and the boat could not get out to them, they were reduced to tins of corned beef and dry goods: golden syrup, condensed milk and sacks of flour.

Desperate for something fresh to eat, Father ventured down the cliffs to fish. It was during a rare hour of pure sunlight, when the sea sparkled and seals lolled about like fat leeches on the rocks. However, after a seal ripped a fish from his line, Father declared defeat.

Unfortunately, mutton bird eggs were plentiful, and the children gagged as they forced their way through them for breakfast. The mutton birds themselves were also easily got, but the meat was oily and fishy.

Despite Mother doing her best to try to disguise the fishy taste with onions and gravy, there was much plate scraping and pushing of food to the side, even from Father.

After the children finished their lessons with Mother, they were permitted to join Father in the lighthouse again.

When the wind was especially fierce or the rain was blinding white, they held fast to a rope that Father had rigged as a guideline from the cottage to the lighthouse. It was one of the first tasks Father did on arriving.

Mother still lived in terror that the children would be blown over the cliff, and it was true that one time Henry walked out of the cottage only to be knocked flat to the ground by the wind.

At the lighthouse, if they stood too long staring at the sea, they would be told to pick up a paintbrush or help carry a ladder or get moving with the broom!

When they had finished, if the weather allowed it, Father would permit them to walk around the gallery – a narrow deck with an iron railing that surrounded the lantern room.

Because both their parents were kept so busy, once their own tasks were done, the children could enjoy the wild freedom of the island. They explored every inch of the clifftops and admired the great shimmering rainbows that spanned either side, making the island seem like a forgotten fairyland.

Sometimes, they stood with Father at the lighthouse windows while he pointed to a ship on the horizon, or at the telltale white ripple of a whale breaching the water.

On dry nights, Annabelle and Henry lay on a blanket near the cottage and gazed up into the velvety sky, competing for who could spot the most shooting stars.

But just as exciting were the mail boat days. One evening, after an especially rocky flying fox run, the children overheard Father telling Mother the mail boat had brought extra supplies. With winter coming, so too would the storms. Soon, the sea would become too dangerous, and this might be the last delivery run for some time.

Chapter 5

The Storm

Up on the lantern room gallery, Father lowered his binoculars and pointed to the row of lights on a great ship, far off over where the sun was sinking below the horizon. Henry and Annabelle strained to see the ship's golden glimmer. Father then pointed in the other direction.

From across the mainland, a great dark storm was brewing. Savage shreds of grey cloud swirled. Bruised purple lightning flashed inside the clouds, while curtains of rain swept in vertical stripes across the sea. "Looks like we're in for a wild night," said Father.

The children returned with Father to the circular lantern room. There, Father carefully lit the wick and ensured the lens could turn freely before shooing the children away.

"Time for you two to get back to the cottage, or your mother will worry," he said. "Tell her I will be following along shortly. I just have to check that everything is locked down."

The children made it home just as the first gust of rain whipped in, stealing in behind them in a rush of cold wetness as they flung themselves through the cottage door. They did not need to be told by Mother, and went immediately to warm their frozen hands by the stove.

"Sssh!" Mother commanded, pointing to the baby who, for want of a cradle, slept soundly in the nest Mother had made for him in one of the kitchen drawers.

"Father said he will be coming shortly for supper," Henry reported. It was almost impossible to hear him over the fierce wind prising at the brickwork of the cottage, as if desperate to get in. "He has to lock things down."

Mother nodded and ladled soup into their bowls. "Here, warm yourselves with this."

By the time they had eaten their soup, it was pitch-black outside. Still, Father had not come. And all the while, lightning slashed across the island, and the wind hungrily tore and plucked at anything not bolted down.

Mother hummed a song beneath her breath as she washed the bowls, but the children could hear that it was strained.

"How long did he say he would be?" Mother suddenly demanded.

Annabelle looked up from the book she was only pretending to read. "He said he'd be right along!"

Mother waited while the clock ticked for several more minutes, but when it chimed six, she could stand it no longer. She reached for her oilskin coat and pulled a woollen hat flat down, almost to her chin. “I am going to fetch him. Look after the baby. I’ll be back with Father soon.”

"But Mother –" called Annabelle.

It was too late. There was a sudden *whoosh*, as if the storm had swept Mother up, and the heavy wooden door slammed shut behind her.

Chapter 6

The Light Goes Out

The baby turned restlessly in his nest of blankets and Henry shushed him back to sleep. There was no point in trying to read by the fire – both children were too unnerved by the sudden thumps and bangs as the storm prised at the buildings. Each child glanced nervously at the clock as the minutes ticked by.

"Do you think we should see where they are?" Annabelle finally suggested.

"Mother said we were to wait and look after the baby," Henry replied. "She said she'd be back with Father."

"But that was ages ago," Annabelle replied.

Henry chewed his lip.

"And listen," Annabelle added, "the storm has died down."

It was true, the windows had stopped shaking. Outside, it was almost eerily calm.

Annabelle wiped at the fogged-up window with her sleeve. "Henry, quickly! Come look!"

Henry rushed to join her at the window.

The two turned to stare at each other. A terrible thing had happened. Instead of the familiar sweep of the lighthouse's beam, there was nothing ... only darkness. The light had gone out!

The children layered on coats and boots and, with Annabelle casting a last glance at the sleeping baby, they flung themselves into the darkness with only a single lamp between them. They felt for the rope, still miraculously attached to the cottage, and stumbled their way along the line.

The lighthouse door was open and the air that ran up the spiralling staircase was icy.

With the metal steps so wet and slippery, the children did not dare run. They had been warned often enough by Father that a single missed step could break their necks.

As they reached the top, they saw that the lantern room was completely dark. A broken windowpane showed where the wind had gusted through and blown out the flame in the lantern.

Worse still were the unmistakeable lights of the ship out at sea – much closer now than when Father had pointed it out earlier.

“Quickly!” Annabelle said. “We must light the lantern.”

They had seen Father light it so many times before, but now they struggled as the tongue of flame flickered in the cold air that pushed through the black hole where the windowpane had once been.

The lantern stayed lit for the first few revolutions of the lens, but then, as an icy blast swept in, it flickered out.

The children re-lit it. "We will have to stay," Henry said.

"But what about the baby?" Annabelle asked. "And what about Mother and Father?"

Henry pointed to the faint glow of the ship lights out at sea. "The baby will have to wait. We have to keep the light burning or all those people out there could die."

"I still think Mother will be very upset with us," Annabelle said. She took a deep breath. "I'm going to fetch the baby." She added hopefully, "Maybe Mother and Father will be back in the cottage."

But they both knew this was unlikely. If their parents had made it back to the cottage, they would have come to find them by now. Besides, they too would have noticed that the light had gone out – the worst possible thing for a lighthouse keeper to let happen.

Chapter 7

Save the Ship!

Annabelle cautiously felt her way down the spiral staircase. They only had one lamp and she had left it with Henry so he could see to relight the lantern if it went out again. She tried not to think about the awfulness of slipping and tumbling into the dark hole of the stairwell.

Down by the door, Annabelle felt for the rope hooked to the outer wall and fixed her eyes on the dim glow of the cottage window ahead.

Behind her, the periodic sweep of the lighthouse beam told her that Henry was managing to keep the lantern lit.

Inside the cottage, the fire had died down. The air had a fierce nip and the baby was crying.

"Mother? Father?"

There was no reply.

Annabelle scanned the room for any sign of her parents having returned, but there were still only two washed and stacked soup bowls on the bench, and the oil lamp on the table burned low.

Annabelle gently lifted the baby from the open drawer and tied him to her, as she had often seen Mother do, with the red shawl that hung on the hook. She thought for a moment, then reached into the cupboard below for a can of condensed milk and a can opener, and tucked them into her large skirt pocket.

Back outside in the dark, Annabelle stumbled towards the lighthouse. The light above faltered, before resuming its steady course.

She clanked her way up the twisting metal steps, the baby seeming to become impossibly heavy. When she reached the lantern room, she was panting with the effort.

All night, the children took turns re-lighting the lantern when the wind blew it out. Annabelle opened the condensed milk and they dipped their fingers into the creamy sweetness for themselves, then offered a finger for the baby to suck on. When it became too cold to sit for long, they walked around and around the lantern.

They did not mention Mother or Father once. Neither could bring themselves to voice their greatest fear. If a cow could be blown over the cliff, then what about a grown man or woman?

When the first grey light of dawn stole through the darkness, the children wearily nodded at each other. They had kept the light burning. Their reward was to see the great ship safely pass by to the other side of the island, away from the treacherous rocks.

The baby was sound asleep, his little rosebud mouth searching dreamily for more condensed milk.

Annabelle let out a great yawn. “We did it,” she said.

Henry nodded. “We kept the light burning.” And then, because it could be avoided no longer, “Where you do you think Mother and Father are?”

Annabelle’s face paled and her voice diminished to a whisper. “I don’t know.”

Chapter 8

We Raised Them Right

In the cold light of day, the awful question Annabelle and Henry had both avoided was now plainly out there between them. Ordinarily, there would be nothing that could have kept their parents from them. Nothing that would have stopped Father from keeping the lantern lit. So, along with tearing at buildings and smashing glass, what other damage had the storm done?

They descended the stairs, around and around, almost hypnotised with exhaustion.

Outside, they saw the true extent of the damage. The roof of a shed had been torn off and flung part-way across the island where it now lay, its trusses exposed and twisted into a bizarre angle. The heavy wooden shutters on the cottage had been half ripped off their hinges.

Further down, where the fuel shed was, they saw that the door had been wrenched off. And in the doorway lay a pair of boots. A pair of boots connected to legs …

The children dashed to the fuel shed.

Inside the fuel shed, Mother had their father's head cradled in her lap. She glanced up wearily, as if only just waking. Father's head was bound with a torn-off strip of her apron, and at his forehead was a bloom of browning blood.

There were tears in Mother's eyes as she reached for the children. "I had to stay with him," she whispered. "I was afraid he would not make it to see the day."

It was a long and slow process, helping to carry Father up to the cottage, and required many stops. When they laid him on the sofa, Mother asked Annabelle to heat some water.

As Mother gently sponged the great cut on his forehead, she told the children, "Head wounds usually involve a lot of blood. But it looks worse than it is. Your father will have a scar like a pirate."

When Father awakened, he seemed surprised to see them all ringed about him. "I have work to do," he said, attempting to struggle from the sofa, only to fall back again in exhaustion.

"What happened?" he finally asked.

"You were hit by a flying piece of roof iron," Mother told him. "I found you knocked out on the ground and had to drag you into the shed to shelter from the storm. You really never know what will come around the corner."

As if it all came back to him, Father's eyes widened. "But the lighthouse? A pane of glass was smashed. I had to fetch another pane to fix it. Without it, the light would have gone out."

The full horror of it now dawned on him. "That ship last night ..."

Mother could not let him suffer any longer. She gazed proudly at Henry and Annabelle. "Your children," she said softly. "Our children. We raised them right. They will be able to do anything in life." She smiled. "They kept the light burning, Robert. All night long. They kept the light burning."